H. Montgomery Hyde at his home in Tenterden, Kent in February 1981 aged 73

H. MONTGOMERY HYDE

ULSTER UNIONIST MP, GAY LAW REFORM CAMPAIGNER AND PRODIGIOUS AUTHOR

Jeffrey Dudgeon

Belfast Press

Published by Belfast Press
56 Mount Prospect Park
Belfast
BT9 7BG

First published 2018

Typeset in Adobe Garamond Pro 11

ISBN 978-0-9539287-9-8

Author's Biography

Jeffrey Dudgeon MBE was the winning plaintiff in 1981 at the European Court of Human Rights at Strasbourg in a case against the British Government. This resulted in the decriminalisation of homosexuality in Northern Ireland in October 1982 and was the first successful gay human rights case in Europe. He is the author of *Roger Casement: The Black Diaries with a Study of his Background, Sexuality, and Irish Political Life* (2002), second edition, 2016, also *Roger Casement's German Diary 1914–1916* (August 2016). All publications are available on Amazon and in Kindle form.

He was elected in 2014 an Ulster Unionist member for the Balmoral DEA of Belfast City Council.

Jeff presented his Montgomery Hyde working papers to PRONI in 2008 and some US copy material in 2015.

Tel (028) 90664111 or 079 2125 1874
jeffreydudgeon@hotmail.com

Jeff Dudgeon in his GMB room at Trinity College, Dublin, in 1968, reading Montgomery Hyde's Penguin book on Oscar Wilde's trial

H. MONTGOMERY HYDE

It will be surprising to many, and perhaps distressing to some, that the Member of Parliament who led the campaign to have the House of Commons debate the Wolfenden report[1] – let alone implement it – was an Ulster Unionist MP, Harford Montgomery Hyde.[2] He was to pay a heavy political price for his bravery.

---

[1] A short version of this work was given as a paper on 30 June 2007 at the Wolfenden50 conference in King's College, London under the title *H. Montgomery Hyde, the Ulster Unionist MP (and author of The Other Love) who led the 1950s Westminster campaign for homosexual law reform and his struggle for political survival*. The conference commemorated the 50th anniversary of the Report of the Departmental Committee on Homosexual Offences and Prostitution (better known as the Wolfenden report, after Sir John later Lord Wolfenden, the chairman of the committee). It had been published in September 1957. The committee was set up in 1954 by the Conservative Home Secretary, Sir David Maxwell Fyfe and came after several well-known men, Lord Montagu of Beaulieu, Michael Pitt-Rivers and the journalist Peter Wildeblood, were sensationally convicted of gross indecency and jailed. Fyfe, later the 1st Earl of Kilmuir, was to be an ardent opponent in the House of Lords of the Sexual Offences Bill which eventually in 1967 decriminalised consenting homosexual acts, in private, only in England and Wales and only if they involved two men over the age of 21. It is said he never imagined the committee would favour law reform which it did with only a minority of one. Wolfenden's son Jeremy, it transpired, was gay although it is reckoned his father was not aware of it at the time. The *Belfast Telegraph* published a 1,500-word version of the conference paper on 14 August 2007 to commemorate Hyde's birth centenary on that date.

[2] Confusingly, 'Montgomery' was Harford Hyde's second Christian name (and mother's maiden name). Increasingly people took it to be his primary Christian name. In the manner of the times, Hyde only used 'H', his first initial, on publications, not Harford which was the

The debt owed to him has gone largely unremarked, although he would be recognised by many as the author of that, still fresh, history of homosexuality in Great Britain and Ireland, *The Other Love*[3], perhaps his most memorable and long lasting work. With its rich and detailed narratives, "fusing legal knowledge with illustrative anecdotage,"[4] it is still the best book on the subject. Interestingly, Antony Grey,[5] secretary of the Homosexual Law Reform Society (HLRS) provided case histories and cuttings from the society's files for its contemporary section. It remains the definitive book on British homosexual history written in a racy no-holds-barred style with original accounts of lives lived as sexual outlaws.

Hyde was to be the author of nearly fifty books.[6] Although

---

name his family and friends called him.

[3] *The Other Love: A Historical and Contemporary Survey of Homosexuality in Britain,* London 1970. It was published in the U.S. under the title *The Love That Dared Not Speak Its Name.* Another, far less substantial work by Hyde on some of the same themes is his 1987 book *A Tangled Web: Sex Scandals in British Politics and Society.*

[4] Dictionary of National Biography (DNB) entry.

[5] Antony Grey was the pseudonym of Anthony Edgar Gartside (A.E.G.) Wright (1927-2010) and the key gay campaigner in the 1960s in the Homosexual Law Reform Society (HLRS). None of the other major figures in the campaign were themselves gay. The Albany Trust was a charity set up alongside the HLRS "to promote psychological health in men through research, education and social action." In 2008, Anthony published a personal and family memoir, *Personal Tapestry,* in an edition of 100 copies. It includes letters from and to his Ulster ancestors who migrated to Manchester in the 1820s telling of high casualty disturbances in Co Armagh and Glenoo, Co Tyrone.

[6] Other books in the enormous Hyde oeuvre of over 50 titles include those on T.E. Lawrence entitled *Solitary in the Ranks*; on Edward Carson (thought by Dr Ian Paisley to be the best of the three Carson

H.Montgomery Hyde

An Historical
and Contemporary
Survey of
Homosexuality
in Britain

THE
OTHER
LOVE

Front cover of Hyde's The Other Love

Penguin Crime 3/6

Famous Trials 9:
Roger Casement

H. Montgomery Hyde

he wrote rapidly he was a consistently thorough and accurate historian. Some of his biographies were written to order but it was those works on a spying or sexual topic (both subjects where secrecy was involved) to which he devoted most attention and effort. His publications on intelligence and defence matters however nearly outnumber those with gay themes. He also wrote innumerable articles and book reviews.

There was another anniversary to be celebrated in 2007, related to the Wolfenden report, and that was the 25th anniversary of the passing of the Northern Ireland Order in Council on 25 October 1982 which brought the Ulster law into line with the then 15 year-old England and Wales reform of 1967.

I must be one of a now, small number of people who actually attended some of the parliamentary debates at Westminster from 1965 to 1967, actually in 1966, in the House of Lords, when I was an eager 20-year-old wishing to meet other gays, not knowing where to find them, and very afraid to ask. This was despite being happy in my homosexuality. I have ruefully gathered since that some gay supporters of the HLRS were also present in the public gallery but I did not notice them or recognise some might be there.

2007 was also the, largely unmarked, centenary of Hyde's birth. Born on 14 August 1907, his background was Belfast merchant class while his secondary schooling was in England at a Yorkshire public school.[7] His father, James Hyde was a

---

biographies); on air raid defence policy between the wars; *Strong for Service* on Lord Nathan, Attlee's Aviation minister; also on Rufus Isaacs, 1st Marquess of Reading, Viceroy of India, and the Lord Chief Justice who presided at Roger Casement's trial. (See bibliography below.)

[7] Hyde won a scholarship to Sedbergh College in Yorkshire having earlier attended Mourne Grange preparatory school in Kilkeel, Co. Down. According to former Belfast city councillor John Harcourt, the Mourne

linen merchant and Unionist councillor for Cromac.[8] The
family were living at 16 Malone Road in Belfast according to
the 1911 census. Although his mother Isobel was said to have
come from a Protestant Home Rule background, her father
Harford Montgomery being "a Gladstonian", all were involved
in the 1914 UVF gun running. He attended Queen's University,
Belfast where he gained a first class history degree, and then
Magdalen College Oxford and a second class law degree.

So why did Hyde take up this deeply unpopular struggle?
Did he have a political death wish? Indeed who was he and
what happened to him?

Married three times, he was on the surface an unlikely
champion of homosexual law reform so why the exceptional
interest in the matter? And how was it that what is now reported[9]
to be the most homophobic place in the western world, and was

---

Grange headmaster spoke of being so impressed by Hyde at the age of
nine reading Gibbon's *History of the Decline and Fall of the Roman Empire*.
[8] James Hyde, an auctioneer and linen merchant, was a councillor
for Belfast Corporation's Cromac ward and was involved in the UVF
gunrunning in 1914 when weapons were landed at Bangor near the
family's then Cultra home. Hyde although only seven, recalls being
"used as a dummy casualty so that the women could practice first aid
on me." (*Belfast Telegraph* interview 18 January 1977)
[9] *Love Thy Neighbour: How Much Bigotry Is There In Western Countries?*
Vani K Borooah, University of Ulster and John Mangan, University
of Queensland; January 2007. "Northern Ireland has the highest
proportion of bigoted people in the western world…Homophobia
was by far the main source of bigotry in most western countries: over
80% of bigoted persons in Northern Ireland and Canada and 75%
of bigots in Austria, the USA, Great Britain, Ireland and Italy would
not want homosexuals as neighbours." The dubious nature of this
poll's results is exemplified by the fact that Canada equalled Northern
Ireland in the level of homophobia of its bigoted people. Perhaps the
respondents here and there are just more honest.

then certainly, highly conservative, produce, elect and tolerate such a public representative?

The further question in most minds must be: Did he have gay relationships? His own words on that subject were, "My feelings were always distinctly heterosexual."[10] He certainly knew gay people, particularly at Oxford, as he recorded, although he was older than most of his fellow students. There he occupied Oscar Wilde's rooms[11] which apparently concerned his father who feared he might follow in his footsteps. He later even shared a room in MI5 with Guy Burgess, the diplomat, Soviet spy and defector, whom he described as "a thorough going homosexual and hard drinker with a distinct dislike of washing." Antony Grey believed the notion of any gay affair highly unlikely but describes him as "a highly-sexed man and interested in all aspects of the subject."[12]

When first in London, Hyde had a regular Belfast correspondent, Ronnie[13], who had been at Queen's University

---

[10]　None the less, all the classic markers of gayness were there: an interest in history, archives, genealogy and spying, an affection for aristocracy, the ownership of two ginger marmalade cats and a tendency toward Rome. Only church music was absent.

[11]　"I developed hepatitis due to the severe cold [?] and was advised to get warmer accommodation. I chose rooms over the college kitchens. I didn't know at the time they were Wilde's. That was when my interest in Wilde began." (*Belfast Telegraph* interview by Michael McDowell, 18 January 1977).

[12]　Email to writer 15 July 2007

[13]　PRONI D3084/B/B/2/1. Ronnie wrote to Hyde from a house named *Royton* in Marlborough Park North, Belfast. His surname is not given in the letters. In the Hyde papers in Austin, Texas there is a letter from a Ronnie Wathen, dated 6 August 1964, discussing Casement's sexuality. It starts "Dear Monty" and continues in an intimate vein. He writes from Athens and speaks of his own recent life

with him. His letters reveal something of their lifestyle, love
affairs and modern outlook. For example, Ronnie wrote in May
1930 of a girl he had frightened, with talk "notably of sapphism
and v.d. of which she knew enough to be mortally scared."
On 27 March 1931, he asked archly of (I presume) condoms:
"If you want some more merchandise let me know. The last
lot must have done yeoman service by this time or else your
laundry is very kind to the washable variety. I hope they never
starch them by mistake."

As to religion, Hyde wrote, "For a time, I admit I was
greatly attracted to the Roman church, especially the ritual,
so much more appealing to my aesthetic sense than the dull
Protestant services. But already at Queen's I was beginning to
have doubts about all religious beliefs."[14] He stated in a 1972
BBC programme that he had fallen in love with a Catholic girl
at Queen's. This lack of religious belief enabled Hyde to break
from many related conformities. In the House of Commons,
he always affirmed, instead of taking the oath but this, he said,
was never noticed back home.

---

being "dramatically heterosexual" and of the imminent birth of a child
by an "Icelandic girl Asta Kristinsdottir living with me on Permanent
Loan." Mention is made of receiving a copy of the Casement trial book
from Hyde in Karachi. Wathen's life dates were 1934-1993 so he may
well be a son of Hyde's Belfast friend. Also an R.J. Wathen of Wilton
Place, Dublin writing about Casement in 1961 in a letter to *Threshold*
describes himself as a young Englishman living in Ireland and a friend
of Hyde. He says he agrees with "Peter Wildeblood's moral distinction
between a homosexual and a paederast." See also the reference in
Bill McCormack's 'Roger Casement in Death' (pp. 212-3) where he
describes Wathen as an "English poet and mountaineer", saying he
took issue with Hyde against the diaries' authenticity arguing instead
for the Normand authorship.

[14]   PRONI D3084/A/5B

Studio portrait of a young Montgomery Hyde

Harford Montgomery Hyde's graduation from Queen's University, Belfast in 1928

He looks like a matinee idol in his 1930s studio photographs, yet earlier, at his graduation, more of a young fogey.[15] He was 5' 7" tall and appears to be a classic 1920s person; somewhat louche, having lost his virginity to a prostitute in Italy, according to his own memoir. He seems to have been influenced and shaped politically by becoming an adult in that brief Roaring 20s decade of prosperity and freedom between the wars. One journalist describes him as "a rake."

Hyde was called to the Bar in 1934 working briefly in London and on the North East circuit. His first salaried employment was with the 7th Marquess of Londonderry whose wife Edith was a famous London political hostess and whose influence on Ramsay MacDonald was held by some to be suspect.[16] From 1935–39, Hyde was librarian and Private Secretary to the Marquess in his 'appeasement' period, hired specifically to research the family papers and write its history.

---

[15]   PRONI D3084/A/3 and D3084/B/A/2

[16]   Lady Londonderry, according to Ulick O'Connor, called Hyde 'Monty the Mole' because "he was always burrowing after things," adding she was "very into the Irish Literary Revival. Yeats and Gogarty wrote her letters." During a hot August weekend in 1970, hosted at Mount Stewart by her daughter, Lady Mairi Bury, O'Connor describes bathing in its sea water pool: "Monty dives in and swims with quite an impressive trudgeon stroke, up and down." He quotes Hyde ("He never looks at you straight. Closes his eyes as he encounters yours") describing his initiation into the Freemasons as "frightening and solemn" and explaining that one of the reasons he lost his "seat was that he had said King Billy was fond of the boys." (*The Ulick O'Connor Diaries 1970-81*, pp. 41-46). Lady Mairi Bury, who resided in Mount Stewart until her death in November 2009, had 1930s recollections of Hyde. In conversation with this writer, she was most concerned with mistakes he made in his books on her family and his description of himself as her father's secretary when he was that for only one week, otherwise he was the librarian and someone who had 'spilt red ink on the carpet.'

His works on the family included *Londonderry House and its Pictures*, and *The Londonderrys: A Family Portrait. The Rise of Castlereagh*,[17] a remarkable book for 1933, which remains very highly regarded, showed Hyde's liberal tendencies. It is reckoned his most enduring historical work.

Lord Londonderry had been a Northern Ireland Education Minister in the 1920s, famous for trying to integrate schooling. He was later Air Minister in the MacDonald and Baldwin cabinets, and who, against the progressive or parsimonious view, heightened the RAF's budget and encouraged the early development of radar and the Spitfire. He built the airfield in Newtownards near his family seat which was bombed by the Luftwaffe in the Easter Tuesday air raid of 15 April 1941 with the loss of 13 young soldiers' lives.[18] Hyde always defended Londonderry whose entertainment of Ribbentrop[19] at Mount

---

[17]   Lord Castlereagh, Robert Stewart, the 2nd Marquess of Londonderry, b. 1769, was Foreign Secretary from 1812 until he committed suicide in 1822, due to a sudden severe depression. In a paranoid state, he told King George IV he was being accused of homosexual activities, as he put it, the "crime of the Bishop of Clogher." He, Percy Jocelyn, a son of the 1st Earl of Roden, had recently been charged after being caught in a compromising position with a guardsman, John Moverley, at the White Hart public house in Westminster on 19 July 1822, and deposed as Bishop in October after fleeing to Scotland. Hyde also wrote *The Strange Death of Lord Castlereagh* which Lady Mairi Bury advised this writer was inaccurate and overstated, relying, as it does, on a mid-century story to explain Castlereagh's suicide over a blackmailing incident in 1819 with a transvestite male prostitute.

[18]   They were mostly local lads from the 70th Battalion Royal Inniskilling Fusiliers who were guarding the site. The Belfast Blitz consisted of two huge air raids in April and May 1941, in and around the city, with the loss of one thousand lives and huge destruction in the centre, north and east of Belfast.

[19]   Count Joachim von Ribbentrop, later German Foreign Minister,

Stewart and his meeting with Hitler haunted him politically until his death.

In 1939, Hyde married Dorothy Mabel Crofts from Cheshire, an artist and linguist, later a vendeuse running a fashion shop in London. The Dublin raconteur and Senator, Oliver St John Gogarty proposed the toast at the London wedding.

Lt. Col. Hyde, as he became, and was so addressed throughout most of his parliamentary career, had a good war, mostly in intelligence but he continued writing and publishing. He first served as an Assistant Censor in Gibraltar in 1940, was then commissioned in the intelligence corps and engaged in counter-espionage work in the United States under Sir William Stephenson, Director of British Security Co-ordination in the Western Hemisphere.[20] He was also Military Liaison and Security Officer, Bermuda from 1940 to 1941 and Assistant Passport Control Officer in New York from 1941 to 1942. He was with British Army Staff, USA from 1942 to 1944, attached to the Supreme HQ Allied Expeditionary Force in 1944, and then seconded to the Allied Commission for Austria until 1945. After the war, he became assistant Editor of the Law Reports until 1947 and was legal adviser to the British Lion Film Corporation, then managed by Alexander Korda, up to 1949. And in 1948 he published *Trials of Oscar Wilde*, a precursor of three more Wilde books published in many editions.[21]

---

was then Ambassador in London. In 1935, he negotiated the Anglo-German Naval Agreement. He was hanged in 1946 after a trial in Nuremberg for war crimes. Hyde attended Goering's trial at Nuremberg and that of Gary Powers in Moscow.

[20] Sir William Stephenson's biography was written by Hyde and published in 1962 as *The Quiet Canadian*.

[21] The four Wilde books were *Trials of Oscar Wilde* (1948, Penguin 1962); *Oscar Wilde – A Biography* (1962); *Oscar Wilde: the Aftermath* (1963); and *Lord Alfred Douglas* (1984).

The background to Hyde's political career in Northern Ireland is that Ulster Unionist MPs took the Conservative whip at Westminster, tended to be aristocratic, officer class or barristers, and were largely left to their own devices. Prior to the 1972 reform, key power and patronage was at local government level, particularly Belfast Corporation and not at Stormont. The Unionist Party was a Protestant all-class alliance, more of a movement than a party. It had started as something of a broad church but was ossifying by the 1950s, although remaining hyper-democratic in structure. The Unionist government mirrored the welfare state and NHS reforms of the 1940s.

The British Labour Party had declined to take members in Northern Ireland or organise there since 1918 so the Ulster Unionist Labour Association and the Communist Party of Northern Ireland seized the Labour franchise, leaving no outlet for genuine progressives and trade unionists, Protestants in particular, to this day. And no purpose in politics except sectarianism.

Hyde had planned a parliamentary career since the 1930s and actively scouted for seats. However the war intervened, postponing any election from 1940 until 1945. He then applied for the South Belfast Unionist candidature and was unfortunate enough to miss the nomination by one vote. Five years later, North Belfast was to select him.[22] He could have

---

[22]   Hyde's nearest rival for the North Belfast candidature was Brian McConnell, later a Stormont MP, and a life peer from 1995 until his death in 2000. Hyde feared that his earlier listing of King William III, Prince of Orange, as a homosexual might come back to hurt him at this selection meeting. It did, but later. His somewhat unconvincing and unused crib, in 1950, was that he was only quoting another author. Rev Ian Paisley, a member of North Belfast Ulster Unionist Party in Dock ward in the 1950s, recalled when First Minister, to this writer, his proposing a motion to Grand Lodge condemning

a Penguin Book 4/-

Famous Trials 7
Oscar Wilde

H. Montgomery Hyde

Sir Compton Mackenzie with Harford Montgomery Hyde MP unveiling a blue plaque in October 1954 at Oscar Wilde's home, 34 Tite Street, Chelsea

expected to hold his seat for a quarter of a century or more. In the event, he represented the constituency for just nine years. His maiden speech was on the uncontentious subject of the unenforceability of Northern Ireland maintenance orders[23] in Great Britain, and the consequent problem of border hopping husbands.

He was a UK Delegate to the Council of Europe Consultative Assembly in Strasbourg from 1952 to 1955, majoring on simplifying European visa and border controls. He was also an incessant traveller, a visit in 1958 to East Germany and Czechoslovakia getting him into difficulty with political exiles when he lamely defended himself saying, "There are terrible things going on. Cultural matters are a safe subject in common."

In 1954, as the foremost author on the subject, he presided over the unveiling of a London County Council plaque to Oscar Wilde at his home in Tite Street in Chelsea. In 1956 he argued successfully for the preservation in legislation of Trinity College Dublin's copyright library status. During the 1950s, he wrote a regular column in the *Empire News* and *Sunday Chronicle* newspapers, and much other journalism.[24]

Hyde for suggesting King William was a homosexual. Paisley cut his political teeth in the fight to get rid of Hyde in the North Belfast Ulster Unionist Association.

See also an *Irish Times* letter of 5 June 2007 from James McGivern about Rev Ian Paisley's son's attack on homosexuals: "Should we not judge Ian Paisley jnr by his actions rather than his words? Surely every July 12th, he, and indeed his dad, dress in gaily coloured clothes and regalia and honour that great homosexual – King Billy. Is this not definitive proof that Mr Paisley can hate this sin but still do his duty as Northern Executive minister and love the sinner?"

[23] The Maintenance Orders Bill

[24] There is little Hyde broadcast material extant. BBC NI has, at Cultra, a radio arts programme, *Studio Three*, broadcast in September

Contrary to concerns expressed at home, he did involve himself in Northern Ireland affairs, despite properly realising he was sent to Westminster, to be a United Kingdom MP. In the economy debate on the Queen's speech on 12 November 1957, Hyde managed a rare break in the convention that the province's internal affairs were not discussed in the House of Commons, which ban was due to the existence of a parliament at Stormont in Belfast.

In the section on productivity, he drew attention to Ulster industry's difficulties, which he said were not least due to the credit squeeze and the fact that "overdraft rates are still higher in Northern Ireland than they are across the border in the Republic of Eire." This was an issue remarkably similar to

---

1976, on Oscar Wilde. Introduced by Portadown-born gay film critic Alexander Walker, the participants included Sheridan Morley and Micheál MacLiammoir as well as Montgomery Hyde. He mentions how Lord Alfred Douglas, who, by then, had "abjured homosexual behaviour", having become a Roman Catholic, contacted him at Oxford. They dined and Douglas later gave him some memorabilia, which Hyde said "started me off as a Wilde collector." He added that Wilde and Bosie's life together had not been continuously criminal since "both preferred young boys, as opposed to each other." Hyde's voice is pleasant on the ear, upper class but not grating, and with hardly a trace of a Northern Ireland accent. Cultra and BBC Motion Gallery (motiongallery@bbc.co.uk) have a networked 1972 radio programme featuring Hyde. This is in the *Self Portrait* series (ref.34767 (1)); the script is in PRONI (ref. D3084/A/5B). It remains vibrant and easy to listen to. He briefly mentions his part in the homosexual law reform campaign in Parliament, describing it as "modest," and saying that the reform did not apply to Northern Ireland. There is also a brief TV interview with Hyde in 1959 on the government's release of the Casement diaries. On 6 January 1955, Hyde appeared in an edition of the BBC political discussion programme, *In the News,* the first Ulster MP to do so.

THE ACT OF 25 HENRY VIII
CHAPTER 6

Le Roy le veult

'*Forasmuch as there is not yet sufficient and Condyne punishment apoynted and limited by the due course of the Lawes of this Realme for the detestable and abominable Vice of Buggery committed with mankind or beast . . . that the same offence be from henceforth adjudged felony and such order and form of process therein to be used agaynst the offenders as in cases of felony at the Common lawe. And that the offenders being hereof convict by verdict confession or outlawry shall suffer such paynes of death and losses and penalties of their goods chattels debts lands tenements and hereditaments as felons being accustomed to do accordynge to the order of the Common Lawes of this Realme. . . .*'

This measure, first enacted by Parliament in 1533, made homosexual acts an offence under English criminal law. With the exception of the penalties of death and forfeiture of property, for which life imprisonment was substituted in 1861, the Act remained in substance on the Statute Book until 1967.

Reproduced by permission from the original in the House of Lords Record Office.

Le Roy le veult ('The King wills it') is reprinted from The Other Love

the current debate on corporation tax rate differentials, north and south. He also blamed a combination of civic disturbance and general economic problems, this being the second year of the IRA's 1956-62 campaign, pointing out "there have been more than 200 incidents caused by illegal organisations resulting in damage in excess of £600,000." He alluded to the high number of unemployed in Northern Ireland amounting to "more than 29,000 people or 6.2% of the total number of insured employees."

His earliest gay-related parliamentary intervention[25] was a question tabled on police agent provocateurs after the acquittal in 1954 of Weng Kee Sam, a young Singaporean. He and another man, Frederick Beauchamp, who committed suicide before the trial, had been charged with gross indecency at Gloucester Road tube station. Weng Kee Sam later successfully sued the British Transport Police for £1,600 for malicious prosecution.[26] The Home Office strenuously denied Hyde's suggestion of provocateurism when police carried out such "distasteful duties" said to be "essential to the preservation of public order and decency."[27]

---

[25]   Dr R.B. McDowell (b. 1913), an acquaintance and fellow Ulsterman and Unionist, albeit at TCD where he was Junior Dean, felt Hyde's involvement in homosexual law reform was socially as well as politically unwise. "I can't see Harold Nicholson leading a gay parade. Well-bred people got on quietly with their lives then," he told the writer in his Trinity rooms on 30 August 2007.

[26]   *News of the World*, 5 February 1956. This and many other relevant cuttings were provided by the Lesbian and Gay Newsmedia Archive (LAGNA) at Middlesex University. My thanks are due to Robert Thompson (r.e.thompson@mdx.ac.uk) and the Hall Carpenter Archives for supplying them: see http://hallcarpenter.tripod.com/lagna/cuttings.htm

[27]   *The Other Love*, p. 210-11

1st October, 1967

THE CASEMENT PAPERS

Sir, -- There may have been some confusion due to the
fact that two members of the Bigger family served at
different times in the Irish Senate, Sir Edward Coey
Bigger, who died in 1942, and his son, Professor Joseph
Warwick Bigger, mentioned by Mr. Frank MacDermot
(September 30). It appears that the Professor was his
father's informant about the destruction of the Casement
papers by the antiquarian J.F. Bigger of Ardrigh, and
not the other way round as Mr. MacDermot suggests.

I have it on good authority that at, or shortly
before, the time of Casement's capture and execution,
Professor Bigger, then a medical student living with his
parents in Dublin, went to stay with his uncle the
antiquarian in the north. During this visit he was shown
the papers consisting of several diaries and also a number
of compromising letters from homosexual correspondents.
After talking it over with his nephew, the antiquarian
told him that he thought the best thing to do was to burn
the lot, which he accordingly did. On returning to
Dublin, young Bigger immediately reported to his father
what had happened.

With all due respect to Mr. MacDermot, I still
adhere to the view that the late Mr. J.J. Horgan first
heard the story from the elder of the two Senators, whom
he knew well, but that it was only after it had been
corroborated in detail by the son, in the course of a
chance meeting in the University Club, Dublin, some years
later, that Horgan was convinced that the surviving diaries
were genuine. Of course, this does not in any way detract
from my acceptance of Mr. Rene MacColl's account of the
matter, which initiated this correspondence.

Yours faithfully,

The Editor,
The Times,
London, E.C. 4   H. Montgomery Hyde

*Montgomery Hyde unpublished Times letter on F.J. Bigger's destruction
of diaries 1 October 1967*

4th September, 1967

Dear Mr. French (or is it Professor?),

Thank you very much for taking the trouble to write
to me about my letter to <u>The Times</u>. What you say confirms
the feeling I have always had since I first heard the story
from Rene MacColl that F.J.Bigger destroyed the Diaries and
other papers left with him by Casement. But I find it
difficult to believe that he should have done this before
1916. After all, he kept Casement's clothes. Why should
he not also have held on to the Diaries? That is not to say
that the late Professor J.W.Bigger, his nephew, did not
stay with him two years previously, but if F.S.Bigger showed
him the Diaries I am surprised that he should not have
mentioned the writer's identity. Casement was very wellknown
by reason of his exposure of the rubber atrocities in the
Putamayo for which he was knighted and he already had an
international reputation, although only known to a small
circle for his Irish Nationalist sympathies.

Rene MacColl has gone to Vietnam for his newspaper but
I will certainly show him your letter when he gets back as
I know he will be most interested.

Many thanks again for writing.

Yours sincerely,

H. Montgomery Hyde

R.B.D. French, Esq.,
Newtown Verney,
Kilternan,
County DUBLIN, IRELAND

*F.J. Bigger destroys the diaries - Montgomery Hyde to R.B.D. French 4
September 1967*

He first debated the question of Casement's diaries in the Commons on 3 May 1956 when the junior Minister, William (later Lord) Deedes declined to depart "from the (government's) policy of silence,"[28] and again on 2 May 1957 when the Home Secretary, R.A. Butler only admitted that certain "confidential documents" of Casement's existed. Butler was still not prepared to explain their nature and declined even to say if any diaries existed. This debate led to Hyde starting an extensive, 20-year correspondence with all the proponents and opponents of the diaries' authenticity, their letters duly responded to, typed and neatly filed. He also wrote two substantive pieces in the *Sunday Times* in April 1957 on the Casement controversy, which made the MP's interest in the subject of homosexuality plainer in Belfast.

In July 1959, the Home Secretary was asked again about the Casement diaries when Hyde called for the Home Office both to admit they existed and to allow the public to see them. As Singleton-Gates's book, replicating some of them, had just been published, limited access to view them was then granted.[29] The fact that there were five, not three, diaries then first emerged. The erotic fifth diary only became available in this writer's 2002 book *Roger Casement: The Black Diaries with a Study of his Background, Sexuality, and Irish Political Life* (2nd edition 2016)[30], as its publication had previously been threatened with

---

[28] Hansard, Commons Debates. Vol. 552, cols. 749-60. Deedes argued that verification of the diaries' existence and granting access would be unfair, as Casement, due to his execution, was now unable to answer the allegations involved!

[29] The Casement author, Roger Sawyer, recalled to this writer (in 2007) Herbert Mackey, the doyen of the diary forgery theorists, telling him the preposterous story that Hyde was having an affair with R.A. Butler, which explained the decision to release the diaries.

[30] The less controversial *Roger Casement's German Diary 1914-1916*

an obscenity prosecution.

After Wolfenden's publication, the House of Lords on 4 December 1957 was the first to debate the report on a motion proposed in its favour by Lord Pakenham (later the Earl of Longford). It was not taken to a vote.

On 21 May 1958, Hyde came second in a Commons ballot for notices of motion and announced he would call attention to the Wolfenden Report in three weeks. The day before that debate, and backed by Hyde, Desmond Donnelly[31] (who with Bob Boothby[32] in 1953 had called for a Royal Commission "to investigate the law relating to the medical treatment of homosexuality") pressed the government to allow enough time. The Home Secretary prevaricated; so on 13 June, Hyde was required to propose that the House "took note of the report of the Departmental Committee on Homosexual Offences and Prostitution."

Hyde stood up, and said he begged to move. He only managed 37 words: "I regret that there is not more time to develop the subject. I hope that in the minute that is left to me I can express the opinion that this is a most valuable social document and —". The Speaker then cut him off.

The next day the remarkably modern looking, *Daily Mirror* headline was 'ONE MINUTE'. The accompanying, supportive

---

edited by Jeffrey Dudgeon was published in August 2016.

[31] Desmond Donnelly, the independent-minded Labour MP for Pembrokeshire, was later a rebel against Harold Wilson's steel nationalisation plans and ultimately joined the Conservative Party. He committed suicide in 1974.

[32] Bob, later Lord Boothby, was the long-time lover of the then Prime Minister Harold Macmillan's wife Dorothy, and was himself reputedly gay. Like Liberace, he was none the less successful in winning libel damages of £40,000 from Mirror Newspapers in 1964 over an accurate accusation in relation to his association with the Kray twins.

article read, "It is nine months since the Wolfenden Committee made their recommendations. The Committee took three years to collect their evidence…and one minute [was] given to the subject yesterday." And so the matter disappeared off parliament's timetable for a further six months. This courageous minute was to be Hyde's political undoing.

In November 1958, when the government relented and allowed a debate, Hyde contributed a half-hour speech which was wide-ranging and thoughtful, and covered both aspects of the report. He concluded by demanding equality for the homosexual and the prostitute. Earlier he quoted a letter from a consenting adult who had been gaoled and released, only to be informed on again, losing his new job. He pointed out "three popular fallacies that have been exposed by the Report"; that "male homosexuality always involves sodomy"; that homosexuals are "necessarily effeminate" and that most relevant court cases "are of practising male homosexuals in private." Only one hundred men a year, he said, were convicted of sex in private with consenting adults.

These ideas, novel to the wider public in 1958, can be directly traced back to the 1890s works of Havelock Ellis and J.A. Symonds. The final government speaker David Renton[33] concluded definitively, unlike Butler, saying, "We believe it is the instinct of most members of the public and most members of both Houses of Parliament to decline the Wolfenden proposal." Decriminalisation was now shelved for a decade.

Reports of Hyde's speech at home were not extensive. *The Belfast News Letter* did title its story as 'Montgomery Hyde in Wolfenden debate', but reported his remarks after the comments of R.A. Butler and Labour's front bench spokesman Anthony

---

[33] Lord Renton of Huntingdon, one time National Liberal MP, died on 24 May 2007.

Greenwood who said there is "no justification to impose legislation on homosexuals." Hyde's reading of a letter from a homosexual was quoted, as was his warning against dropping the legal requirement to prove annoyance by prostitutes before conviction.

Ironically on 26 November 1958, the day of the Commons debate, Ian Harvey, the Conservative MP for East Harrow, resigned both as a junior Foreign Office Minister and as an MP, being gazetted as Steward of the Manor of Northstead.[34] On 11 December, he was in court charged with an offence in St James's Park against public decency and was fined £5 as was his partner of the night, Coldstream Guardsman Anthony Plant.

Hyde had been asked in 1950 by David Ogilvy, a colleague from MI6, to make contact with "my old fag from Fettes days, now an MP for Harrow and another admirer of yours. Name is Ian Harvey."[35] He was later to become a vice-President of the Campaign for Homosexual Equality (CHE).[36]

But such seriously liberal views had already begun to pull Hyde down along with the traditional complaint that he did not visit the constituency sufficiently often. He was also a convinced abolitionist on capital punishment and was a co-sponsor with Sidney Silverman in 1956 of a bill to abolish hanging. It passed in the House of Commons only to be defeated in the Lords.[37] *Tribune* picked him out as one of four key players in

---

[34] A device appointing an MP to an office of profit under the crown thus compelling them to vacate their seat.

[35] PRONI D3084/A/7

[36] CHE, one of Britain's first gay organisations, flowered in the 1970s. H. Montgomery Hyde and Peter Hain were to become two of its honorary Vice-Presidents.

[37] The reverse happened with the Earl of Arran's 1965 Sexual Offences Bill which passed first in the House of Lords. Humphry Berkeley's Bill which succeeded in getting a 2nd reading in the Commons fell due

that first success. Indeed, he was drifting toward Labour, as he had presciently begun to doubt the wisdom or efficacy of the Unionist Party's rigid alliance with the Conservative Party. Ironically Hyde also successfully moved an amendment to which Silverman agreed, excluding Northern Ireland because of its devolved status (presumably also to try to stop antagonistic Ulster MPs voting). He pointed out however that in the previous twelve years there had been no executions in the province. And only eleven since partition.

The Belfast newspapers reported extensively on Hyde's considerable attempts in early 1959, the general election year, to stem opposition to his reselection, On 6 January, he addressed the Shankill branch's AGM. Questioned for two hours on the death penalty and the Wolfenden report, he said, "I believe I have the support of the Shankill. I have threshed capital punishment out with my constituents before and they know my views." On 8 January, he was noted in the *Belfast Telegraph* as a Suez rebel, apparently the only time he voted against the whip. Next day he averred, "I must plead guilty to being the best known of the Ulster MPs." Although accepting he was a Suez rebel, Hyde said he thought subsequent events had proved him right, adding, "My primary interest is the prevention of crime and the treatment of offenders."

Henry Holmes, the Shankill's Stormont MP, defended

---

to the calling of the 1966 general election when he lost his Lancaster seat to Labour. He blamed his defeat on the Bill. Although the average swing in 1966 (3.5%) was against the Conservatives, that against him was nearly twice that in an adjacent seat. Turnout in his constituency was also untypically high. Berkeley believed from canvass returns that Conservative voters were also abstaining significantly thus allowing a Labour victory by some 1,800 votes rather than a near dead heat. Leo Abse, a Labour MP, then took up the parliamentary torch on law reform.

him saying, "Although he has sponsored one or two unpopular causes I do not believe these are sufficient grounds for discarding him." His opposition to the death penalty, and his support of the Wolfenden recommendations on homosexuality and prostitution were all declared to be non-party matters.

Hyde was heavily backed in the English liberal press, with favourable editorials in *The Guardian* and *The Sunday Times*. There was however little or no controversy in the letters columns of the Belfast papers about his progressive views. Licensing law was then the biggest controversy not gay law reform. However, Robin Bailie, later a Stormont MP, in a rare letter of 11 December 1958 did call on the church to stick to preaching morality and leave law making (including that on homosexuality) to men. There was no apparent response.

A few weeks after Hyde's speech in the Commons, and in the absence of any hope of law reform, Northern Ireland's police and prosecutors accelerated their work of rooting out gays for on 18 December 1958, nineteen Lurgan men were charged with gross indecency "and other charges involving indecency."

Their cases were heard before Lord Justice Curran[38] at Belfast Winter Assizes. Before sentencing seven of them to terms of imprisonment, he remarked, "Cries of repentance after an act had been committed was no new thing in his experience."

"You seem to have been a cancer in the society of Lurgan," said Curran when sentencing William Wells aged 64 who was "not professionally represented" to three years in prison. Of the

---

[38] Interestingly, Lord Justice Curran's daughter Patricia had been murdered in November 1952 in a case where there were rumours of a homosexual connection between her brother and the young airman, Iain Hay Gordon, later convicted of her murder (and since acquitted on appeal). Gordon was known to have had gay contacts in Belfast and Co. Antrim.

remainder, six were gaoled for a year: Thomas Burton 30, lorry driver, George Haddock 43, optical lens maker, George Hunter 27, engineer, "now living in London," Edward Stevenson 38, unemployed, James Walker 30, packer, and Thomas Kerr 52, labourer. Of those bound over, James Robinson 32, a grocer was defended by E.W. Jones MP (later Attorney General) with a plea that he was liable to mental illness. This was accepted by the judge who said he was treating Robinson as a special case, declaring, "You have had a week in prison and you know what it is like. I hope it will make some impression on your mind."

The other ten[39] were given recorded sentences and also bound over. Thomas Jenkinson 23, linesman, denied the offence, pleaded not guilty and was acquitted. He said he had only made a statement to keep police from approaching his girl friend and family. The crimes were not described except in his case, where he had initially stated "an incident took place at the entrance to some garages." The police claimed to "have three witnesses to prove it." The judge commended the police officer concerned, Detective Constable Ernest Drew, saying, "I think you have done a very useful piece of work in cleaning up this mess in Lurgan." Antony Grey wrote that "the offences came to light through the police interviewing each of the accused in

---

[39] The other ten, very ordinary martyrs bound over were George Wilson, 44, clerk; William Sharpe 55, TA watchman; Howard Thompson 44, fitter; David McKinley 44, hotel employee; George Fleming 48, packer; John McCappin 58, clerk; Thomas Neill, 52, weaver; William Magill 65, old age pensioner; William Taylor 44, power loom tenter; and William Dowds 32, unemployed.

They were indeed martyred, as in the words of the Earl of Arran, on 21 July 1967, when his Bill finally became law: "My Lords, Mr Wilde was right: the road has been long and the martyrdoms many, monstrous and bloody. Today, please God! sees the end of that road" (quoted in *The Other Love* p. 268).

turn and getting him to implicate one or more of the others."[40]
What seemed unusual in this trial were the sheer number
charged and the severity of the sentences. However not much has
changed in relation to such small town round-ups, exemplified
by the 2006 Coleraine events, when a dozen men were convicted
and publicly shamed (with their houses and cars duly attacked,
and marriages blighted) for trivial cottaging offences. Such
trials studded the English newspapers in the 1950s, but
extensive group arrests and prosecutions[41] continued to be an
Ulster peculiarity, perhaps indicative of an institutionalised
homophobia in the police, prosecution and judicial system.

Under the radar, opposition was building to Hyde's
Wolfenden and Casement activities which unfortunately only
muddied already troubled waters so far as his constituency
association was concerned. In the event, he faced a challenge
for the parliamentary nomination from Air Marshall Sir George
Beamish, once an Irish rugby international.

The MP went to the Unionist Party selection committee

---

[40] *Quest for Justice* p. 38-9

[41] Ironically, in 1893 the first prominent person convicted of gross
indecency under the 1885 Act, and preceding Oscar Wilde, was a
fellow Belfast MP and Orangeman, Edward de Cobain (1840-1908).
He was sentenced to 12 months' imprisonment with hard labour in
1893 after fleeing in 1891 first to Brussels and then to New York (see
The Other Love p. 137-8). De Cobain, a deeply unpleasant individual
according to his correspondence in the National Library of Ireland
(NLI) was a religious hypocrite and relentless hypochondriac who
complained his sister "has made home a perfect hell" (NLI MS
17,729). His accusers gave evidence as to his groping and sexual
talk, while one Benjamin Rosemond, a telegraph boy, witnessed to
attempted buggery on him at de Cobain's residence, Hampton House
on Belfast's Ormeau Road where he called seeking a reference for a
job. (PRONI ANT/1/2C/3/30 and ANT/1/2A/5 pp. 24, 245 & 249)

meeting on 12 January 1959 armed with a letter of endorsement from Edward Carson's widow (which looked and read suspiciously as if he had written it himself). The vote was 70 for Hyde, 60 for Beamish and 12 for David Carlisle. After his elimination, it was 77 to 72, a five vote win for Hyde, a result "greeted with prolonged applause." Reselection with nearly 150 voting was a remarkable achievement given the worrying publicity. This defeat knocked Sir George out of the running. Hyde's enemies however fought on.

The ratification meeting, normally a formality was on 13 February 1959, but Hyde was in the West Indies on what was described as an "industrial" West Indies parliamentary committee tour of the Caribbean, "to promote trade and business contacts."[42] A local news story ominously read, "in the event of the association rejecting Hyde against whom there is some feeling in the constituency the matter will be considered again."

Unwisely, Hyde chose not to cut short his trip and thus missed the full North Belfast Imperial Association ratification meeting in the Belfast YMCA. Despite pleas from his wife and certain Belfast friends, he chose instead to appeal to the chairman, Mr David McClelland, for a postponement.

That plea was in vain as McClelland was already hostile. He simply replied, "Wire received. Regret you cannot attend meeting. Must go on. Management Committee decision." Writing letters, from a hotel in Kingston Jamaica, to his number one enemy in wintry Belfast, the association secretary Mrs Noble who thought him "a bad man[43]" was also bordering on

---

[42] Other such trips included one to St. Helena and another to Sikkim where "the Crown Princess tried to persuade me to become a Buddhist."

[43] Recollection of former Belfast Councillor John Harcourt, in conversation with this writer in May 2007.

the politically insane.

In a much bigger turnout, and by 171 votes to 152, Hyde's reselection failed to be ratified. By 19 votes, the Unionist Party lost its one respected voice at Westminster and abroad, and the only MP who ever advised his people of changing times, while attempting to modernise and moderate Unionist opinion. Unionism's failure to send a consistently liberal voice to Westminster since remains a dangerous deficiency that has done it considerable damage, not least with Labour governments.

The *Belfast Telegraph* reported, "Mr Hyde's rejection is a result of criticism amongst constituents over his attitude over certain problems particularly the Wolfenden report, capital punishment and the return of the Lane pictures to Ireland; further there was a feeling he did not visit the division sufficiently." One view expressed was that as the vote was so close he might have carried the day, had he been present.

Two days later, now in Belize City, Hyde complained that it was a "rank discourtesy holding the meeting without him," especially as there were 3,000 members in the constituency. His wife in London the next day said, "I shall advise him to cut out the rest of his tour if that is possible and deal with the matter on the spot." She had however written earlier to him in Jamaica: "SO THAT'S THAT. I'm sorry darling perhaps it's for the best. No more politics. No more Belfast politics. Oh bliss." He did make efforts to have the decision overturned by Unionist Party headquarters on procedural grounds but he had no high-level political support.

Although he had made little secret of his progressive views during the capital punishment debates, the campaign for access to the Casement diaries and his writings on Oscar Wilde, Hyde's political undoing was his parliamentary interventions and outspoken views on the decriminalisation of homosexuality.[44] Ironically, if he had managed to effect the Wolfenden report recommendations at Westminster, the reform would not have applied in Ulster. In the event, the 1967 England and Wales Sexual Offences Act was not extended to Northern Ireland until October 1982, by a vote of 168 to 21 in the House of Commons. This was only after my 7-year European Court of Human Rights case succeeded a year earlier, vindicating Hyde's efforts of a quarter of a century before.

With Stormont back up and running, intermittently, the 'no change; no reform' policy prevailed again, most recently in relation to equal marriage but earlier on adoption and the blood donation ban. This obviously started with the Rev Ian Paisley, leader of the 1977 *Save Ulster from Sodomy* campaign, becoming the DUP First Minister in a coalition with Sinn Fein in 2007. An interesting exception is the then DUP First Minister, Arlene Foster, getting the Assembly in 2016 to permit Westminster to extend legislation to Northern Ireland on gay pardons and disregards. This was a first for the DUP in not opposing, indeed enabling a gay law reform.

Hyde vacated his seat at the election in October 1959[45], not standing as an independent as had been mooted, and despite having received many letters of support from within North

---

[44] In an *Irish Times* interview of 5 January 1985, Hyde stated, "In fact Lord Boothby and I really initiated the whole thing and started the Wolfenden committee – the [Unionist Party] caucus said 'we cannot have our member condoning unnatural vice'. That was it. That really finished me."

[45] The 1959 North Belfast general election result was Stratton Mills (UU) 32,173, Jack McDowell (NILP) 18,640, and Frank McGlade (Sinn Fein) 2,156 (loses deposit). The previous result in 1955 was H. Montgomery Hyde (UU) 33,745, Billy Boyd (NILP) 15,065, Frank McGlade (Sinn Fein) 4,534.

Belfast, including a number from his "Hebrew constituents," as he put it, and beyond. There was (and is) a folk view that the North Belfast Unionist Association at that time was conducted out of the Synagogue, explaining to a degree its apparently liberal approach, although no such aspect to the dispute surfaced in the press. The one (anonymous) antagonistic letter in the Public Record Office of Northern Ireland files, and postmarked Worthing, stated "Ulster has no time for an advocate for homosexuality." It also accused him of "gallivanting in the sunshine."[46]

When he took up these controversies he was not as strapped for cash as he was later to become. His wife pointed out that, but for the fact he was a year short of the ten years necessary (at that time) to secure a parliamentary pension, losing his seat had compensations.

Hyde was particularly beset by money problems, his divorce from his second wife Mrs Mary Eleanor Bennett née Fischer[47] in 1966 putting him under great financial strain due to the alimony settlement. His first dissolution in 1952 from Dorothy Crofts had not been costly as it was amicable, she taking up with another intelligence man, Wilfred "Biffy" Dunderdale[48] of MI6. She admitted adultery in writing in court, their professional co-respondent who had apparently also acted for Wallis Simpson, later Duchess of Windsor, being indisposed. Hyde managed to keep his first divorce out of the Belfast newspapers, only

---

[46] PRONI D3084/I/A/2

[47] She was the daughter, born in India, of Colonel L.G. Fischer of the Indian Medical Service. They married in July 1955 at Caxton Hall registry office in London. The *Belfast Telegraph* cuttings library has an excellent picture of the couple at that wedding which was used in their 14 August 2007 birth centenary article.

[48] Wilfred Dunderdale is said to be a key component in the genesis of Ian Fleming's character, James Bond.

telling his Unionist Association at the time of his remarriage. This apparently passed without comment as it was by then "a fait accompli."

The costly divorce explains the books written to order[49] and the rapid sale of associated papers once a volume was published. He had already been obliged to sell his considerable collection of Oscar Wilde papers in 1960 for $30,000 (some given to him by Bosie). They would now be worth millions. He married lastly in October 1966, Rosalind Roberts (Robbie), née Dimond. She had no connection with Northern Ireland prior to her marriage to Hyde but became more outspoken in her Unionist views than Hyde himself.[50] They had briefly been colleagues at British Lion in the late 1940s when she was Sir Alexander Korda's secretary. She was said to have been Hyde's secretary for some twenty years.

After losing his seat, Hyde became Professor of History and Political Science at the University of the Punjab in Lahore in 1959 taking the opportunity to research on Ulstermen who had worked in the Simla Hills and elsewhere in India.[51] Later

---

[49] Alistair Cooke (now Lord Lexden), at that time in QUB's Institute of Irish Studies, who assisted Hyde in PRONI research on de Cobain recalls, in June 2007, "In answer to the question why he wrote so many books he said 'alimony, dear boy, alimony'."

[50] Mentioned in conversation in 2007 with Anthony Malcomson, former Chief Executive of PRONI, who arranged the deposit of Hyde papers. He has added that the Hydes visited Belfast regularly in the 1970s and 80s, staying with the late Diana Hyde, his sister (who was in the SDLP), or at Mount Stewart with Lady Mairi Bury. Alistair Cooke adds, in 2007, "His lively third wife made him happy and more relaxed than would otherwise would probably have been the case."

[51] PRONI D3084/M/C/1 (Lahore cuttings). One example was Brigadier-General John Nicholson, a somewhat bloodthirsty Lisburn man who led the assault on Delhi during the 1857 Indian mutiny

in a letter to *The Times* he was to condemn the 1971 massacre of students at Dacca University by the West Pakistan army. Hyde earlier said he had "not given up hope of returning to Westminster perhaps at a by-election,"[52] but it was not to be, and neither did a suggested university posting to Nigeria come to pass. Writing was his only career and income thereafter, although from 1958-61, he was an honorary Colonel of the Northern Ireland Intelligence Corps (Territorial Army).

His involvement in progressive and controversial issues did not cease. He continued his work opposing capital punishment.[53] He also published two articles in May 1965 in *The People*[54] to further advance the cause of homosexual law reform. The second entitled *The Million Women,* appeared after the House of Commons had rejected Leo Abse's first Bill, showing "itself more reactionary than the Lords," as he stated. That article dealt with lesbians whose "association" was not regarded as an offence, and "Sappho the poetess who wrote passionate verses about the lovely maidens who gathered round her."

Abse, a Welsh (and Jewish) Labour MP[55], after a vote under

---

[52] PRONI D3084/M/C/1

[53] Capital punishment was finally abolished in Great Britain in 1965.

[54] These articles apparently "brought a torrent of letters asking for help, many from working class homosexuals" (see *Coming Out* by Jeffrey Weeks p. 182).

[55] Leo Abse, in a letter to this writer of 20 July 2007, states that although he has "no recollection of meeting him in the few years that our parliamentary service co-incided" does recall Hyde joining him and Chapman Pincher, the journalist, at lunch at the Café Royal. There he describes Hyde being "exploited and used by Chapman Pincher who advanced over the meal, his wild conspiracy theories; with these Hyde passively concurred," Abse thinking as he left "how

and was mortally wounded. His statue was later moved to the Royal School Dungannon, prompting a Hyde article.

the 10 minute rule on 5 July 1966 giving him leave to introduce
a Bill, was finally successful in effecting homosexual law reform
in July 1967[56] after being given government time by the Labour
Home Secretary Roy Jenkins. Later, Hyde noted dryly, "As usual
the Northern Ireland Members, including my successor,[57] went
into the Noe Lobby."

He appeared as a witness for the defence in the *Fanny Hill*
and *My Secret Life* obscenity trials, and for the other side in the
successful 1966 prosecution of *Last Exit to Brooklyn* by Hubert
Selby jnr. This earned him the lifelong enmity of its publisher
John Calder. That verdict was overturned on appeal in 1968.

Harford nervously slipped a fortnight's entries of Casement's
erotic 1911 diary into the 1964 edition of his 1960 book on

---

very sad it was to see a man who had lived a noble parliamentary life
reduced to being little more than a 'slave' to such an unwholesome
man." Leo Abse died the next year in 2008.

[56] Barbara Castle MP wrote of Monday, 3 July 1967 in *The Castle
Diaries* (1984): "All-night sitting on the Sexual Offences Bill. It was
a good job I stayed, tired as I was. At one stage we only carried the
closure by three votes. Trailing through the lobby at 4 am, I ran into
Lena Jeger who put her arms round me and said in a piercing voice,
'Aren't we good, doing our bit for the boys!' She really is a joy." Lena,
later Baroness Jeger, died in 2007. Leo Abse is quoted in a well-
excavated article by Geraldine Bedell in *The Observer* (24 June 2007),
saying, "On my 90th birthday, I had lots of telegrams. I never had
one word of thanks from any gay activist or lobby. When I've shown
any reservations about the gays, they haven't forgotten."

[57] *The Other Love* p. 266. Hyde's North Belfast successor, Stratton
Mills MP, was voting against decriminalisation in England although
the Bill did not even apply to Northern Ireland! Antony Grey's *Quest
for Justice* (London, 1992) gives the best account of law reform's ten-
year parliamentary process, with the heroes and villains well described.

Roger Casement's trial[58], which ensured it was banned in the Irish Republic. Regardless of the impression that the outlawing of the first-ever extract from Casement's most sexual diary would give, the Censorship Board ploughed on in its task of protecting the Irish people from sex and smut. In that month's blacklist, Hyde's book was joined by Alex Comfort's *Sex in Society* and Dr R. Swoop's, *The Expert Way of Making Love*. Apart from sex manuals and diaries, the Board also put a series of racy novels to the sword; *Cage of Passion* by I.C.A. Mari, Babe Deal's *Night Story*, and *The Wayward Wench* by Noel de Vic Beamish. Only Mike Baldwin's *A World of Men* had a whiff of homosexuality.

Penguin Books appealed for a revocation of the prohibition but the application was dismissed. None the less, the Censorship of Publications Appeal Board decided to refund the £5.0.0 deposit lodged and accordingly enclosed a Payable Order for that amount with its letter of 14 October 1964.

Oddly, the Penguin edition was dedicated to Michael Francis Doyle, "of the American Bar, defender of Sir Roger Casement no less after his execution than during his trial". Doyle had diametrically opposed views to Hyde on the authenticity of the Casement diaries while Hyde seemed suspicious initially that Doyle had run off with the large sum of John Devoy's money ($5,000) he was supposed to hand over in London for the defence fund. Hyde, who interviewed Doyle for the book, failed to draw any malign conclusion from contradictory evidence as to its eventual disbursement. However Casement's meticulous solicitor, George Gavan Duffy, never accounted for any American money despite Doyle telling Hyde he gave the cheque to him. This was done after he had seen Casement to get it endorsed and that he had then been given £250 of it by Gavan

---

[58]   *The Trial of Sir Roger Casement,* Hodge 1960; *Famous Trials 9: Roger Casement,* Penguin paperback edition 1964

Hyde electioneering in 1955 in the "mean streets" of North Belfast and being garlanded with a lucky black cat mascot (PRONI).

Duffy. Hyde asked to see the receipt but Doyle said he could not locate the "photographic copy of the check".[59] In several pages of his book,[60] perhaps disingenuously, Hyde explained how it was difficult to understand Gavan Duffy's concerns about a lack of funds, given the American money.

Hyde sold the bulk of his Casement documentation, both books and manuscripts to an Irish antiquarian dealer in 1970. In a letter to the Casement author, Roger Sawyer, he wrote, "I no longer have the considerable collection of Casement material which I amassed over the years", not mentioning that this was his usual practice with such papers once he had mined a subject

[59] Michael Francis Doyle to Hyde, 4 November 1958, Series 1.23 Harry Ransom Humanities Research Center Austin, Texas
[60] *Funds for Casement's Defence*, Appendix 1, pp. 183–185

to exhaustion. It also provided further income for a man who, as he said "never had much money and always spent what I've made, pretty quickly." A purchase from the dealer was later made by Professor Roger Louis of the University of Texas at Austin. All that remains in PRONI is the correspondence that came after the disposal, apart from the sale catalogue itself.

There is now nothing available in the way of original material to illuminate the discovery in the National Library of Ireland (NLI) of Casement's evocative and revealing poem *The Nameless One*. Its first appearance in print seems to have been in his *Sunday Times* article of 28 April 1957. There Hyde declared "I have recently been able to examine the Casement papers in the NLI." He suggested that the hitherto unpublished poem by Casement would have "some bearing on the question of whether or not he was a homosexual." Describing what he saw as a "manuscript of a poem by Casement entitled *The Nameless One*", he added, "In my view it betrays strong homosexual feelings in its author." However the manuscript is no longer to be found in the NLI.

Although his Unionism never waned, Hyde blamed the Prime Minister, Viscount Brookeborough[61] for fossilising Northern Ireland in the 1950s, and latterly adopted a New Ireland or federal solution view to the Troubles. None the less, when ambition required it, he had joined both the Orange Order[62] and the Freemasons, saying the one was an essential

---

[61]   Sir Basil Brooke, as was, Prime Minister of Northern Ireland 1943-63
[62]   Hyde joined the Eldon Orange Lodge, LOL No. 7, Clifton Street, Belfast. This is an elite lodge favoured by MPs. See also Wesley Boyd's contradictory articles in the *Irish Times* of 5 June 2001 and 2 June 2004 which are an alternative view from the Ulster left. Boyd quotes in the first a Northern Ireland Labour Party opponent of Hyde, Sam Watt, reporting that at the 1955 election that for all the MP's self-vaunted religious tolerance, he had heard, "loudspeakers mounted on

prerequisite to becoming a Unionist MP and the other an undoubted assistance. In the description of one friend, he was "vain and liked flattery but without being in the least pompous, complacent or self-satisfied,"[63] and someone who felt a need for recognition although several people report he did not always turn up for speaking engagements. He was however awarded an honorary degree by Queen's University of Belfast (QUB) in 1984. Ulick O'Connor recalls his kindness, willingness to help

---

Montgomery Hyde's campaign lorry blaring out the familiar Belfast ditty: 'We'll buy a penny rope/And hang the f——— Pope/On the Twelfth of July/In the morning." Boyd added that Hyde, "lived in Surrey, wrote books and had (for an Ulster Unionist) liberal views on dangerous subjects such as capital punishment and homosexuality. A bon-vivant, he had little concern for the mean streets of North Belfast and looked upon the constituency as a prize that had to be fought for at general elections." In the second version of the article, it is Boyd who reports hearing the sectarian song, this time actually being sung by Hyde: "My first election experience – as a youthful bystander – was in North Belfast...I joined his bandwagon in Alliance Parade. He stood on the back of a lorry with an Orange collarette around his neck, rousing the crowd with a rendition of the [above quoted] familiar Ulster ditty: He won." The truth of who witnessed the matter and who sang the ditty remains unresolved. A photograph in PRONI (D.3084/A/3/12) of Hyde electioneering shows no collarette, rather him being garlanded by enthusiastic 'mean streets' residents with a lucky black cat mascot to set beside his rosette (*see p. 45*).

[63] Assessment of Alistair Cooke, June 2007. Michael McDowell, a former Belfast Telegraph journalist who interviewed Hyde, said of his deselection, "He was 'above' it, he thought. A truly prolific author who worked like hell to pay the bills. I think I wrote that he lacked "charisma" and used that word and he sent me a kind note after the profile saying that the Greek root didn't match with my own definition. He was probably right!"

16 Malone Road, Belfast – the Hyde family residence in 1911

Bertha House, 71 Malone Road – Montgomery Hyde's address in Belfast when an MP

and good conversation.[64]

Hyde working assiduously up to his death on 10 August 1989,[65] just short of his eighty-second birthday, honoured more by a wide readership than by his country. His third wife Robbie survived him. They lived at Westwell House in a flat they owned on the first floor.[66] The house in Tenterden in Kent was once inhabited by Horatio Nelson's daughter. Hyde was earlier a tenant of Lamb House in Rye, once home to his distant cousin, Henry James.[67] Inevitably he wrote a book, *The Story of Lamb House*, about his dwelling. While an MP, his residence in Belfast was given as Bertha House at 71 Malone Road.

He chose in his will a non-religious cremation. "Harford was not a believer," explained the Tory MP Tim Brinton, who

---

[64] Conversation at Ulick O'Connor's Dublin house (30 August 2007) in the gloom of a late summer evening, accentuated by the fact that his electricity has failed some days earlier. O'Connor, a prolific author, sportsman and poet, and unceasing controversialist, described this writer's book on Roger Casement as a biographical masterpiece which on production, as he indicated, was annotated on every page. The comments were however illegible in the dark.

[65] Hyde's *Times* obituary on 12 August 1989 noted that his friends had hoped "he would be given a Life Peerage believing with justification, that he would have made an excellent contribution to debate from the cross-benches." It also described him as "a remarkable and good-humoured raconteur" and a valued contributor to the DNB.

[66] Antony Grey in an email in July 2007, described Hyde as very affable, someone "who delighted in presenting you with signed copies of his books, several of which I treasure. He and Robbie were superb hosts, and my Aunt and I had several memorable visits to both Lamb House and Westwell."

[67] Henry James b. 1843 was the cousin of Hyde's great great grandfather. Henry James's grandfather, William James, was an Ulsterman, born in Co. Cavan. The novelist, Henry, however was no Unionist.

gave the oration at his funeral, although, as he confusingly added, he was an Ulster Protestant.

Under the terms of his will, dated 30 December 1972, such of his political, personal and working papers, in his possession, including an unpublished part-autobiography, were offered to the Public Record Office of Northern Ireland[68] (PRONI) an institution he had helped and supported in a variety of ways since the early 1950s. Eagerly accepted, the important archives were catalogued and made accessible by 1991. The residue of his estate valued at £28,387.00 gross went to his widow after small family-related gifts to his sisters Diana Hyde and Claire Smyth[69]. Robbie was left badly off in cash terms reputedly having to repay the advance her husband had received on his unfinished biography of Walter Monckton.[70] More documents were added to the PRONI deposit after Robbie's death in 1995.[71]

---

[68]   PRONI D3084/A/7. Hyde's partial autobiography was entitled *Leaves of Memory*, but only takes his life up to the early 1950s. His other papers are scattered, with the extensive Casement (and Wilde) documentation largely in the University of Texas at Austin and only the tail in PRONI. Hyde's William Stephenson book material was sold to Churchill College, Cambridge. Oddly, there is little or no 1950s Wolfenden, *Other Love*-related material or constituency correspondence to be found in PRONI.

[69]   Claire had two sons, Peter and Richard, and in 1972 lived at 45 Wellington Park, Belfast. Peter operated Smyth's Irish Linens in Belfast's main street and the city's last linen factory, both now closed. He told me when I tracked him down, co-incidentally, his wife had been secretary to my father when he was manager of the Belfast Bank in High Street. He spoke of how much she appreciated working for him and of his kind nature.

[70]   Anthony Malcomson relates, "She never complained, and used to say 'But we did have some marvellous times together'."

[71]   Rosalind Montgomery Hyde (Robbie) left a gross estate of

In his entry in the Dictionary of Irish Biography, Patrick Maume sums up Hyde as a man who "prefigured later attempts to develop secular and socially liberal forms of Ulster unionism, but also aspired to an older archetype – the raffish clubman despising suburban morals, and delighting in the arcane worlds of the aristocrat, the pornographer, barrister, the prostitute, and the spy."

The gay community, Northern Ireland and the world generally owes a lot to this determined and courageous Ulsterman[72] yet his contribution is largely forgotten or ignored. It is time for him to be remembered.

£130,202 in her will dated 20 November 1991. After many small and large bequests including £500 for the care of their Siamese cat Lottie, Hyde's chair and Book of Service (in the event his framed invitation from the Earl Marshal) at the Coronation of the Queen in 1953 to Dr Anthony Malcomson and £10,000 to the Vice Chancellor of QUB for an annual prize for the top history graduate to be named "The Dr Harford Montgomery Hyde award", the residue of the estate, including presumably book royalties and rights, was left to her husband's nephews Peter Smyth of Belfast and the late Richard Smyth of Guernsey.

[72] The Ulster-Scots term 'thrawn' fits Hyde well. His DNB entry (written by Dr R.B. McDowell) describes him as having "an intense dispassionate interest in the homosexual world" and added he was "diligent, widely and thoroughly read, and assiduous in tracking down manuscript material…his books were carefully crafted and very readable. Though chained to his desk for long stretches he enjoyed congenial company, conversation and his clubs." Dr McDowell then aged 94 (he died in August 2011), recalled in conversation with this writer (30 August 2007) that he first met Hyde in the early 1940s and that they walked in the Dublin hills. An "amusing and vigorous conversationalist" as he recalled, Dr McDowell was impressed on a visit to Hyde's home by his "interesting collection of *Wildeana*" and, in particular, by Oscar Wilde's cellar book.

HARFORD MONTGOMERY HYDE

BIBLIOGRAPHY

The Rise of Castlereagh (Macmillan 1933)

The Russian Journals of Martha and Catherine Wilmot (co-authored with Edith, Marchioness of Londonderry, Arno Press 1934)

More Letters from Martha Wilmot: Impressions of Vienna 1819-1829 (co-authored with Edith, Marchioness of Londonderry, Macmillan 1935)

The Empress Catherine and Princess Dashkov (Chapman & Hall 1935)

Londonderry House and its Pictures (Cresset Press 1937)

Air Defence and the Civil Population (co-authored with G.R. Falkiner Nuttall, Cresset Press 1937)

Princess Lieven (Harrap 1938)

Mexican Empire: The History of Maximilian and Carlota of Mexico (Harrap 1946)

A Victorian Historian: Private Letters to W E H Lecky (Home & Van Thal 1947)

The Amazing Story of John Law: Scottish Financier and Gambler (Home & Van Thal 1948)

Privacy and the Press (Butterworth 1947)

Judge Jeffreys (Harrap 1940; 2nd edition Butterworth & Co. 1948)

Notable British Trials Series, Volume 70: Trials of Oscar Wilde (Hodge 1948); US edition released as *The Three Trials of Oscar Wilde* (University Books, New York 1956); enlarged edition, *Famous Trials 7: Oscar Wilde* (Penguin 1962)

Mr and Mrs Beeton (Harrap 1951)

Cases that Changed the Law (Heinemann 1951)

Carson (Heinemann 1953)

The Trial of Craig and Bentley (Hodge 1954)

United in Crime (Windmill Press 1955)

Mr. and Mrs. Daventry: a Play in Four Acts by Frank Harris, based on the Original Scenario by Oscar Wilde, intro. H.M. Hyde (The Richards Press 1956)

The Strange Death of Lord Castlereagh (Heinemann 1959)

Sir Patrick Hastings; His Life and Cases (Heinemann 1960)

The Trial of Sir Roger Casement (Hodge 1960); *Famous Trials 9: Roger Casement* (Penguin paperback 1964)

Simla and the Simla Hill under British Protection: 1815-1835 (Punjab University Press, Lahore 1961)

An International Casebook of Crime (co-authored with John H. Kisch, Barrie and Rockliff 1962)

Oscar Wilde – A Biography (1962)

The Quiet Canadian: The Secret Service Story of Sir William Stephenson (Hamish Hamilton 1962; US edition released as *Room 3603: The Story of the British Intelligence Center in New York during World War II*, Farrar Straus & Co. 1963)

Oscar Wilde: The aftermath (Methuen 1963)

Norman Birkett, the Life of Lord Birkett of Ulverston (Hamish Hamilton 1964)

A History of Pornography (Heinemann 1964)

Cynthia - the Story of the Spy Who Changed the Course of the War (Hamish Hamilton 1965)

The Story of Lamb House Rye: The Home of Henry James (Adams of Rye 1966)

Lord Reading: the Life of Rufus Isaacs, First Marquess of Reading (Heinemann 1967)

Strong for Service: The Life of Lord Nathan of Churt (W.H. Allen 1968)

Henry James at Home (Methuen 1969)

The Other Love: An Historical and Contemporary Survey of Homosexuality in Britain (Heinemann 1970; US edition released as *The Love That Dared Not Speak Its Name: A Candid History of Homosexuality in Britain*, Little, Brown & Co. 1970)

Their Good Names: A Collection of Libel and Slander Cases (Hamish Hamilton 1970)

Stalin, the History of a Dictator (Hart-Davis 1971)

Baldwin: the Unexpected Prime Minister (Hart-Davis 1973)

Neville Chamberlain (Weidenfeld & Nicolson 1976)

The Cleveland Street Scandal (W.H. Allen 1976)

British Air Policy between the Wars 1918-1939 (Heinemann 1976)

Crime has its Heroes (Constable 1976)

Solitary in the Ranks: Lawrence of Arabia as Airman and Private Soldier (Constable 1977)

The Londonderrys, a family portrait (Hamish Hamilton 1979)

The Atom Bomb Spies (Hamish Hamilton 1980)

Secret Intelligence Agent - British Espionage in America and the Creation of the OSS (Constable 1982)

Lord Alfred Douglas (Methuen 1984)

Crimes and Punishment (Marshall Cavendish 1985)

A Tangled Web: Sex Scandals in British Politics and Society (Constable 1986)

George Blake Superspy (Constable 1987)

Christopher Sclater Millard (Stuart Mason), Bibliographs and Antiquarian Book Dealer (Global Academic Publishers 1990)

The Lady Chatterley's Lover Trial (Regina v. Penguin Books Limited) (The Bodley Head ed. 1990)

Walter Monckton (Sinclair Stevenson 1991)

ROGER CASEMENT
THE BLACK DIARIES

with a study of his background,
sexuality, and Irish political life

JEFFREY DUDGEON

SECOND EDITION
Revised & Expanded

ISBN 978-0953928736

ROGER CASEMENT: THE BLACK DIARIES

The 2nd edition, paperback (and Kindle) version of *Roger Casement: The Black Diaries – with a Study of his Background, Sexuality, and Irish Political Life* by Jeffrey Dudgeon was published in January 2016, the centenary year of the Easter Rising and of Casement's execution.

Extended, and enlarged with a post-1st edition bibliography of nearly fifty new entries, it has 10% more text (728pp.) and a dozen new photographs (ISBN 978-0953928736). A Kindle version (with searchable text and hyperlinked references) is also now available from Amazon.

This second edition includes improved and extended versions of the 1903 and 1910 Black Diaries, and for the month of September in the 1911 Diary and Cash Ledger. New characters are outlined like the Bavarian schoolboy, Max Zehndler, and the Batavian Casement aficionado, Heinrich d'Oleire. The birth name and progressive origins of Casement's mother Anne, a Dublin Protestant, have been ascertained. The ultimate fates of Casement's comrades on the submarine and in Germany – Daniel Julien Bailey, John McGoey, and Adler Christensen are discovered and described. The mystery of the missing money that Michael Francis Doyle brought over from America in 1916 is investigated and solved.

Newly revealed Gertrude Parry and Elizabeth Bannister papers, bought by the NLI in 1952, but never catalogued, have added considerably, since the first edition, to the documentation now accessible in digitised records.

Casement's 1881 *Scribbling Diary* was tracked down by the author in the NLI, within a batch of significant papers that had been catalogued and numbered, but not indexed. The diary was thought lost or stolen since B.L. Reid saw it in the 1970s, and tells more about 'The Sweet Boy of Dublin'.

ROGER CASEMENT'S
GERMAN DIARY
1914–1916

Edited by Jeffrey Dudgeon

ISBN 978-0953928750

ROGER CASEMENT'S GERMAN DIARY, 1914–1916

Roger Casement's German Diary 1914-1916, edited by Jeffrey Dudgeon, was published in August 2016 in paperback (ISBN 978-0-9539287-5-0) and Kindle versions (paperback, 370 pages, unabridged).

This is the definitive <u>unabridged</u> version of Roger Casement's German Diary covering the years 1914 to 1916 when, after the war started, he went to Berlin seeking support for Irish independence. It has 367 pages, over 150,000 words and 45 illustrations.

The German Diary consists of another, and the last surviving, Casement diary, and deals with that most interesting, dramatic and penultimate period of his life in Germany and Berlin prior to his departure to Ireland for the Easter Rising.

It was not a private diary in any sense as Casement left instructions for its future publication. Much of what he wrote was designed to provide a record justifying his time in Germany. He was of an age to have his eye on history while knowing the accusations of treason he had, and would, face, Casement was desperate to have his actions understood. A secondary prompt in the last months was to indicate just how disgraceful and intransigent he felt the behaviour of the Germans had become and how the decision to start the rebellion in Ireland was something he did not agree with for tactical reasons, being an event he hoped to prevent or at least postpone. The final section describes his frantic attempts both to get sufficient arms shipped to the separatist Irish Volunteers and to travel by submarine to Kerry with a view to getting the Easter Rising called off.

The diary and many linked letters give a vivid impression of a man under stress in an alien environment who still manages to observe, describe and appreciate what he sees around him. He writes as an outsider of a nation at war with England and France. His growing frustrations however come to the point where his own mental health is destabilised.

There is a cast of the usual characters that Casement mixed with, political, often aristocratic, although also frequently military men. There were to be none of the street people or lovers that his earlier, more sexual, diaries detailed. In Germany, probably for security reasons and lacking the language, he chose not to go out at night or to cruise for sex. He was also getting on. His Norwegian companion and betrayer, Adler Christensen, looms large, tricking and twisting his way round Germany and America, while draining much of Casement's time and common sense.

The text is laid out in as close a way as possible as the actual manuscripts to provide an impression of the original. The appendices include correspondence and newspaper articles from the time, while bringing the reader up to date with recent articles in relation to Casement in Germany, the Easter Rising and the role of British and German Intelligence, as well as the ongoing Black Diaries authenticity debate which is, if anything, accelerating. That controversy tells of a still contested issue in modern-day Ireland, despite the immense strides made towards gay equality and emancipation, most recently in the Republic.

The diary was in two notebooks in the National Library of Ireland and essentially covers the eight months from July 1914 to February 1915. It begins being written on 7 November 1914 and takes Casement retrospectively from England, to the US and to Germany and then includes a tour of war-torn Belgium. It effectively concludes on 11 February 1915 with him in a sanatorium. At the end, however, there is a brief account dated 28 March 1916 of events later in 1915. Separately, 'A Last Page' picks up the narrative on 17 March 1916 running it to Casement's final days in Berlin.

Casement, a man who wrote too much, drafted many hundreds of other letters and memos when in Germany of which a number of the more significant, particularly those related to the arrangements for his departure to Ireland, are reprinted along with the full, unabridged diary where another writer Angus Mitchell has edited out nearly a quarter of the original text in his book sub-titled *The Berlin Diary*. Those cuts are at times from the most sensitive of areas, including the behaviour of the German Army in Belgium and Casement's increasing disillusionment with the Kaiser's Imperial Government and Prussian militarism. Being complete in its narrative, makes it vastly more readable and comprehensible.

Made in the USA
Columbia, SC
16 April 2018